Katie's Cookbook
Made with Love for My Children

I0106421

Katie Cherry, MS, CHESr, LNHA

STUDIO OF BOOKS
THE SPACE FOR YOUR MESSAGE

Copyright © 2024 by Katie Cherry

All rights reserved. No part of this publication may be reproduced, distributed, or transmitted in any form or by any means, including photocopying, recording, or other electronic or mechanical methods, without the prior written permission of the copyright owner and the publisher, except in the case of brief quotations embodied in critical reviews and certain other noncommercial uses permitted by copyright law. For permission requests, write to the publisher, "Attention: Permissions Coordinator," to the address below.

Studio of Books LLC
5900 Balcones Drive Suite 100
Austin, Texas 78731
www.studioofbooks.org
Hotline: (254) 800-1183

Ordering Information:
Special discounts are available on quantity purchases by corporations, associations, and others. For details, contact the publisher at the address above.

Printed in the United States of America.

ISBN-13: Softcover   978-1-968491-43-7

Library of Congress Control Number:

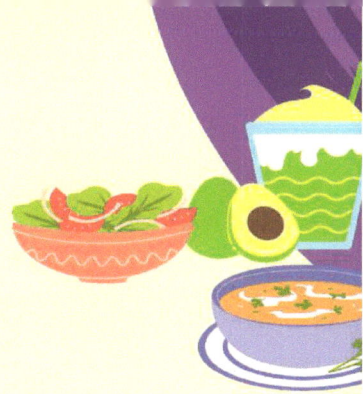

Contents

Side Dishes

Main Dishes

Desserts

Acknowledgments

Thank you to everyone who tries and enjoys these very special recipes! I did not put

all my recipes into this one book; if you want more, please let me know! My

YouTube channel is @KatieDeWerdt. Please like and subscribe!

About the Author

I was born and raised in the southwest suburbs of Chicago. As a very determined young lady, I was the first to graduate from college on my Mom's side of the family. I got an Associate in Arts in 1995, a Bachelor in Community Health Education in 1997 and a Master's in Science in 1998. I also attained a Certified Health Education Specialist certification in 1998. I spent many years in the Healthcare field, where I attained my Nursing Home Administrator license and Food Service Sanitation License. Cooking became a very endearing hobby. I would be watching cooking shows and coming up with fun things to make for my family. In 2023, I attained a certificate degree in website development, and this has allowed me to work on writing this book and several others on the way. I greatly enjoy making people smile. Hopefully, I can bring some of that love to your kitchen.

When I first became a Mom at age 26, that is when I really started experimenting with cooking. I tried to make things that the children would like, but that also had a lot of nutrients. Every one of my friends seemed to be so impressed that my children would eat Tilapia. We probably had that like once a week when my son Matthew and daughter Elora were little. Then, in 2014, I had my son Brent. Things got pretty busy having teenagers and a toddler at the same time. Crock pots are definitely a mom's best friend when you are a busy mom of three, and all of them have somewhere to be. In 2018, my son Matthew was diagnosed with Type 1 Diabetes. This, again, would change our lives and routines forever. About a year after his diagnosis, Matthew and I were talking, and I asked him, "What do you miss most about not being a diabetic?" He said, "Mom, I just want to have a Halloween like before where I could just eat whatever I want and not worry about taking insulin." As you will see, many of the recipes in this are diabetic-friendly. It is very important to me that people understand there is a stark difference between Type 1 Diabetes and Type 2 Diabetes. We were educated by a fantastic group of nurses and doctors. They explained to us that Matthew's immune system attacked his pancreas, and now the pancreas is no longer functional, at which point a person has to take insulin for the rest of their lives. Type 2 Diabetes is when a person

misuses the amount of carbohydrate to physical activity ratio and their pancreas is damaged. Sometimes, this type of diabetes can be reversed with proper diet and exercise. Type 1 can never be reversed. My son has handled being a diabetic with grace and amazing fortitude. I am so thankful for his perseverance. This book is dedicated to all of my children, but especially Matthew, who has barely piped a complaint and has been diabetic for nearly six years.

I have organized this book into three chapters. There are side dishes, main dishes and desserts. I really enjoy cooking for my family. I love cooking for those I love. At Christmas, I have a party where I cook a very large meal for my extended family. This has become a fun event every year. I plan for it almost the entire year, sometimes adding a new dish or item I've learned along the way. For main dishes, I love to incorporate veggies and protein combinations, but not always. These meals are not meant for fufu plates but to feed a family. However, sometimes, I like to plate them beautifully for my eyes.

I have been watching the Food Network for years and have definitely experimented with and incorporated some of the things I've learned there. Thank you to all the superstars on the Food Network for the countless hours of entertainment and the great ideas to incorporate into my own cooking. Thank you to all of my family members who I've watched cook – Grandmas, Mom, Aunts and Uncles.

Years ago, I found an old blank book to write recipes in. I was thrilled because I wanted to write down my family's favorite recipes. On the inside cover, I wrote:

"To my amazing children – Every day that I make food, I pour an extra heaping spoon full of love into it. That is why you love the things I make for you. Please enjoy my recipes forever! Love always, Mom."

So when you're making these recipes, don't forget to add the LOVE. That is the main and key ingredient in every dish.

(It will work best to prepare these dishes by chopping, crumbling and preparing the ingredients list just as they are described in the lists. Prepare before starting the instructions list. Also, make sure to pre-heat your ovens to the degrees specified.)

Side Dishes

Green Bean Surprise

This dish is very simple: Simple ingredients and simple to make, but packs great flavor and healthy nutrients.

2 ½ cups chopped fresh green beans (cut into 1-inch pieces)

1 large white onion (chopped)

3 heaping Tablespoons of Garlic (minced)

5 Roma tomatoes (chopped)

2 Tablespoons of canola oil

1 ½ Teaspoons of Course ground pepper

Salt to taste

1. Combine all ingredients into a large pot.
2. Turn the burner to medium heat.
3. Cook on medium heat until green beans are tender and tomatoes have formed a paste. Should cook for about 45 minutes stirring frequently.

*You can make it ahead of time.

Serves 8.

Dish note: A lot of recipes call for olive oil. Although I do use olive oil often, canola oil is a cheaper and just as healthy option to use instead of olive oil.

Nacho Heaven

This is a super fun side dish. Usually, I make this for the Super Bowl!!

2 taco seasoning packets

1 Tablespoon of taco seasoning (in addition to packets)

1 package of cream cheese (8 oz)

8 Roma Tomatoes

1 can of black olives (15 oz)

1 cup of shredded cheddar cheese

2 ½ pounds of ground beef

2 green peppers (chopped)

1 large white onion (chopped)

Jalapeno pepper to taste (chopped)

2 tubs of sour cream (16 oz)

3 avocados (cut into ¼ inch pieces)

½ cup of lime juice

3 Tablespoons of garlic (minced)

Velveeta Original melting cheese (amount needed will depend on how much you want to make)

1 cup of milk

Salt and Pepper to Taste

Tortilla Chips

All of the following separate sides can be added to desired tortilla chips for Nacho Heaven! Every person can build their perfect nacho.

Meat Mixture:

1. Brown 2 ½ pounds of ground beef. Drain excess grease.
2. Add 1 large onion chopped. Cook for two minutes on medium heat.
3. Add 2 green peppers chopped. Cook for an additional three minutes on medium heat.
4. Add 1 packet of taco seasoning. Add 1 Tablespoon of additional taco seasoning. Mix thoroughly and let cook for another two minutes.
5. Add salt and pepper to taste.
6. Let mixture simmer on medium to low heat, stirring often for 25 minutes.

Melting Cheese:

1. Take ¾ of a cube of Velveeta Original melting cheese. Cut into cubes.

2. Put cubes in a pot with 1 cup of milk (I use whole milk).
3. Heat on low, mixing often until melted thoroughly. Can leave on low heat and mix thoroughly until ready to spread on nachos.

Guacamole:

1. Take cubed avocados (make sure they are slightly soft and ripe), chop Roma tomatoes and mash them with a masher.
2. Add ½ cup of lime juice.
3. Add three Tablespoons of minced garlic. Mash all ingredients together.
4. Add salt and pepper to taste.

Taco Dip:

1. Mix package of cream cheese, 1 tub of sour cream and 1 Taco seasoning packet – can use a blender to mix thoroughly. Layer in bottom of 9 inch round dish.
2. Add half a can of cut black olives on top of the mixture.
3. Add 3 Roma tomatoes chopped on top of the mixture.
4. Add 1 cup of shredded cheddar cheese on top of the mixture.
5. Keep in refrigerator until ready to scoop.

I like to cut some fresh tomatoes and black olives as additional nacho toppings. Also, chopped jalapeno can add a bit of spice to any of these nacho toppings. The extra sour cream tub is also its own topping.

Most items can not be made ahead of time.

Serves 10 people.

Now, you are ready to enjoy nacho heaven. Scoop, splatter, and swish all desired toppings on your tortilla chips. Yum is all I can say.

Green Pepper Pizza

This side dish is great as an appetizer; however, when I'm not wanting a real big dinner, I have used this as my main dish.

3 green peppers (cut into inch strips)

4 Roma tomatoes (cut into circle slices)

1 ½ cups of shredded cheddar cheese

1 ½ cups of shredded fresh parmesan cheese

Garlic Salt to taste (This can be very potent, so make sure you put how much tastes good to you)

1 ½ Tablespoons of dried basil

1 ½ Tablespoons of Weber garlic parmesan seasoning

Spray Oil

¼ cup black olives (cut into circle pieces)

1. Heat oven to 375 degrees.
2. Take a large baking sheet and spray with spray oil.
3. Lay green pepper slices on a baking sheet.

4. Sprinkle garlic salt, dried basil, and garlic parmesan seasoning on green peppers.
5. Bake for 10 minutes.

6. Pull the green peppers out of the oven and add tomato slices on top of the green pepper slices. Before putting it back in the oven, sprinkle again with garlic salt, dried basil and garlic parmesan seasoning.
7. Bake for an additional 10 minutes.
8. Pull out of the oven and add both cheeses and black olives on top of the green peppers and tomato slices.
9. Bake for 5-8 minutes until cheese is at a desired melt.

*Can make ahead of time and reheats nicely.

Serves 3-4 people.

This is full of nutrients and has a great taste, too!!

Spinach Yumminess

This is a dish I usually serve with my large Christmas meal. It is savory and goes well with a large spread of a meal.

1 bag of spinach (16 ounces)

1 large white onion (chopped)

4 pieces of bacon (cooked and crumbled)

4 Tablespoons of canola oil

1 Tablespoon of garlic powder

1 Tablespoon of garlic salt

2 Tablespoons of parsley

1 cup of fresh shredded parmesan cheese

1. Put one Tablespoon of canola oil in a large pan. Add chopped onion and sauté on medium heat until onion starts to caramelize. Mix often.
2. Add three Tablespoons of canola oil and add all of the spinach. Spinach will start to wilt down while cooking. Stir often until the onion and spinach are thoroughly mixed together.
3. Add garlic powder, garlic salt and parsley. Cook on medium heat for 1 minute.
4. Add crumbled bacon and stir thoroughly.

5. Add parmesan cheese and mix until cheese is thoroughly melted throughout the pan. For about 2 minutes, stirring often.

*It does not work well to make ahead.

Serves 4-5 people.

This is one of my favorite vegetable dishes. I've made this with fresh-grown spinach, which gives it a really amazing fresh attribute.

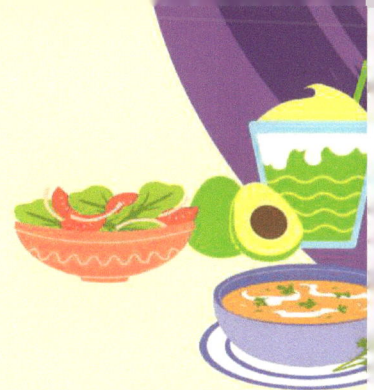

Sour Cream and Onion Mashed Potatoes

This is my youngest, Brent's very favorite potatoes. I make them for him often.

8-10 golden potatoes (peeled and cubed to about 1 inch)

1 stick of butter

10 oz of sour cream

3 Tablespoons of garlic salt (Taste while adding so it's not too salty for your family)

6 Tablespoons of dried chives

Salt to Taste

1. Put peeled and cubed potatoes in a pot of water. Cover water over potatoes. Add two shakes of salt to the water. Boil potatoes until they are soft and can mush against the side of the pot.
2. Drain water from potatoes. Put potatoes back in an empty pot.
3. Put one stick of butter in the center of the potatoes. Use a masher to mash potatoes while butter melts around them. (Some people prefer other methods of mashing potatoes, but this is my favorite because the butter and ingredients mash into the potatoes nicely).
4. Add garlic, salt and chives. Mash additionally until all ingredients are melded.
5. Add 10 oz of sour cream. Mash all ingredients together.

*Can make ahead of time. Reheats nicely.

Serves 7 people.

This dish has become one of our favorite side dishes. I make this for Christmas dinner as well!

Greek Potatoes

This is my take on Greek potatoes. Not entirely traditional, but super yummy. Sometimes, this is great with breakfast foods.

8 Golden potatoes (cut into one-inch cubes)

5 Tablespoons of Cavender's All Purpose Greek Seasoning

1 Large white onion (chopped)

4 Tablespoons of Canola oil

½ cup of lemon juice

1. Put one-inch cubed potatoes, onion, Greek seasoning and canola oil in a large pot. Put the burner on medium heat. Stir consistently and often. Make sure to overturn potatoes at the bottom of the pot often while stirring.
2. You will cook for about 45 minutes until potatoes are soft and all ingredients are cooked thoroughly together.
3. Add ½ cup of lemon juice. Mix an additional minute.

*Can make ahead of time. Reheats well.

Serves 7 people.

My older two children are part Greek, so this is about the only Greek dish I make, but it's another favorite. I also make this for Christmas dinner.

Cooked Carrots

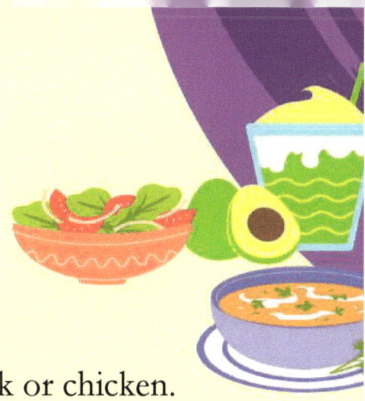

My kids won't eat this one, but I love it. Super yummy with a little grilled pork or chicken.

10 carrots (peeled and cut into ½ inch circles)

½ cup of brown sugar

6 Tablespoons of butter

1. Take peeled and cut carrots and put them in a pot. Cover the carrots with water.
2. Boil carrots until they are soft and the fork can easily push through them.
3. Drain water from carrots.
4. Add brown sugar and butter while still piping hot. Mix thoroughly.

*Can make ahead of time. Reheats well.

Serves 7 people.

This is super simple and easy and adds a nice flare to some great grilling with maybe some rice.

Grilled Asparagus

All of my children eat this dish! Mom wins right here.

6 Tablespoons of Cavender's All Purpose Greek Seasoning

20 Stalks of Asparagus

4 Tablespoons of Canola oil

1. Pre-heat grill to 400 degrees.
2. Use a cookie sheet that you don't mind grilling on. It will get burned and unusable as a cookie sheet in the future. Cover it with tin foil.
3. Put asparagus on a tin foil-covered cookie sheet.
4. Cover with oil and sprinkle the Greek seasoning over the asparagus. (If you have time, you can marinate the asparagus for hours or even one day before – this adds a really great flavor to the dish.)
5. Put a cookie sheet with asparagus mixture on the grill. Mix after about 4 minutes.
6. Cook until there is a bit of char to the asparagus. This usually takes about 10 minutes to cook thoroughly.

*Does not reheat well.

Serves 5 people.

This dish is made often and usually accompanies other grilled dishes, especially in the summer. Yummy!

Main Dishes

Elora and Brent's Chicken Noodle Soup

Some people don't think of this as a main dish, but my son Brent and daughter Elora will eat three bowls each sitting. So, for Elora and Brent, this is a main dish.

1 Whole Chicken

10 whole carrots (peeled and sliced into ½ inch circles)

1 large white onion (chopped)

6 chicken bouillon cubes

1 ½ Tablespoons of basil

3 ½ Tablespoons of oregano

½ teaspoon of sage

Salt and Pepper to taste

16 oz wide egg noodles (cooked with directions on package)

2 Tablespoons of Canola oil

1. Take a large pot. Put raw whole chicken in the pot. Fill with water until the chicken is submerged and the water is over the chicken.
2. Put 6 bouillon cubes in the water.

3. Place the pot on the stove and turn on the heat to high.
4. Add 1 ½ Tablespoons of basil, 3 ½ Tablespoons of oregano, ½ teaspoon of sage and salt and pepper to taste.
5. Put carrots and onion into the pot.
6. Make noodles in a separate pot according to the package. Once the noodles are drained of water, add the canola oil to the strainer and let sit until the soup is nearly ready.
7. Boil the chicken until the chicken is close to coming off of the bone. This varies in time depending on how big the chicken is and how hot your stove boils. Usually, this takes anywhere from 1 hour to 1 hour and 20 minutes.
8. Once the chicken is thoroughly cooked through, take the chicken out of the pot and turn the burner to low.
9. After the chicken has cooled for about 15 minutes, take the chicken meat off of the bone and put it into the pot.
10. Add cooked noodles to the pot.

*You can make this ahead of time. Does reheat well.

Serves 15 servings or more, depending on how big the whole chicken is.

My daughter Elora and son Brent eat bowl after bowl of this simple and delicious soup. It's one of my favorites as well.

Wakey Wakey Eggs and Bacey

My son Matthew named this dish many years ago. We used to make this one very often.

8 Eggs

1 Cup of shredded cheddar cheese

Salt and Pepper to taste

5 Cooked strips of bacon (Crumbled in pieces)

Butter Spray

1. Crack eggs and mix eggs with cheddar cheese.
2. Add salt and pepper to taste.
3. Spray a muffin pan with butter spray.
4. Add bacon to the egg and cheese mixture.
5. Pour egg, cheese and bacon mixture into muffin holes about ¾ of the way full. Eggs will rise when baking.
6. Bake at 375 degrees for 20 to 25 minutes until eggs are baked and have risen nicely in the pan.

*Can not complete ahead of time. Does not reheat well.

Serves 12 servings.

This was a definite favorite in our household for years!

Matthew's Favorite Meatloaf

My son Matthew loves this dish to this day. It is hardy and filling.

3 Heaping Tablespoons of bread crumbs

1/3 cup of whole milk

2 pounds of ground beef

2/3 medium white onion (chopped)

2 Heaping Tablespoons of minced Garlic

1 Large Egg

Ketchup to Taste

Salt and Pepper to taste

1. Line the baking sheet with aluminium foil.
2. Place 3 heaping Tablespoons of bread crumbs in a bowl with 1/3 cup of whole milk. Stir and let sit.
3. Combine ground beef, chopped onion, garlic, egg, ¼ cup of ketchup and salt and pepper to taste. Mix well.
4. Add bread crumbs, and milk mixture to the meat mixture. Mix until all ingredients are infused into the other ingredients.
5. Form the meat mixture into a loaf and place it on the baking sheet with aluminium foil.
6. Brush ketchup on top of the meatloaf mixture.
7. Place in a 400-degree oven for 45-55 minutes.

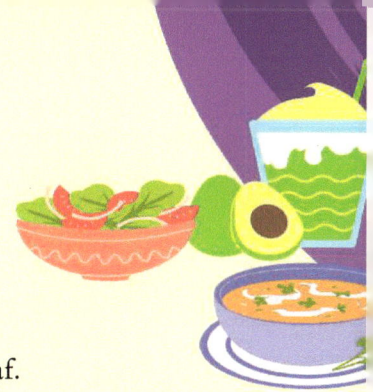

8. Check every 20 minutes and add additional ketchup to the top and sides of the loaf.
9. After the meatloaf is thoroughly cooked through, take it out of the oven and let it sit for about 10 minutes.

*Can make ahead of time and does reheat well.

Serves 5 people.

This has been a dish that our family has enjoyed often as a main dish. Usually, I serve with broccoli.

Beef Stroganoff

My son Brent requested this one this week! He loves it. It's pretty simple to make. I hope you enjoy it.

8 oz of cooked egg noodles

1 ½ pounds of 80/20 ground beef

1 medium onion (chopped)

14 oz can of beef broth

10.5 oz can of condensed cream of mushroom soup

1.25 oz McCormick Beef Stroganoff mix

½ cup of sour cream

2 Tablespoons of Canola oil

1. Prepare noodles according to the package. When completed cooking, put canola oil over the noodles to keep them fresh.
2. In a large pot, brown the ground beef until no longer pink. Use a spatula to break apart beef as it cooks.
3. Add chopped onion and cook for about 1-2 minutes.
4. Add in beef broth, cream of mushroom soup and beef stroganoff mix. Bring to a boil. Then reduce heat to low and let cook for 5 minutes.
5. Remove from heat.

6. Add in sour cream. Mix thoroughly.
7. Add in cooked noodles. Mix thoroughly.

*Can make ahead of time and does reheat well.

Serves 6 people.

This is a great winter dish. It is very filling and yummy!

Amazing Pepper Jack Beef Sandwiches

I've had several people tell me after eating these they only want this beef sandwich from now on. It's a good one. Enjoy!

1 ½ pounds of sliced Black Angus Beef

4 cups of Au Jus

1 Large onion (chopped)

4 Tablespoons of minced Garlic

½ stick of butter

Block of Pepper Jack cheese (shredded)

2 Tablespoons of oregano

2 Tablespoons of garlic salt

Vienna Bread (package usually comes with 6 pieces, but I use them open-faced, so it really becomes 12 pieces)

1. Saute onion and garlic in 1 Tablespoon of butter. Cook on medium heat for about 3 minutes.
2. Put onion and garlic mixture into au jus. Place au jus in a pot on low heat.

3. Take 2 Tablespoons of butter and melt in the microwave. Add 2 Tablespoons of garlic to the melted butter.

4. Take a cookie sheet. Open the bread face up and place it on the cookie sheet. Brush the butter and garlic mixture on the open-faced bread.
5. Sprinkle bread with oregano and garlic salt.
6. Bake bread at 375 degrees for 8 minutes until bread is slightly crusty on the edges.
7. Put sliced beef in au jus mixture. Continue to cook on low while the bread is baking.
8. After the bread is out of the oven, place sliced beef on baked bread.
9. Top the sliced beef and bread with shredded pepper jack cheese.
10. Bake for an additional 8 minutes until cheese is melty.
11. Serve with au jus mixture. I like to take a ladle and pour it over the top of the baked open-faced sandwich. Some may like to just dip in the au jus.

*Can make ahead of time. Does reheat well.

Serves 5 people.

This is a really great way to serve a beef sandwich. My family loves this one.

Super Yummy Meat Sauce with Spaghetti

My daughter Elora inspired this one! She loves spaghetti with meat sauce.

2 Tablespoons of olive oil

2 pounds of ground beef

2 white onions (chopped)

8 cloves of garlic (minced)

2 green pepper (chopped)

56 ounces of diced tomatoes

32 ounces of tomato sauce

12 ounces of tomato paste

4 Tablespoons of dried oregano

3 Tablespoons of dried basil

2 Tablespoons of Kosher salt

1 Teaspoon of ground pepper

Spaghetti Noodles (cooked)

1. Cook noodles according to package. When cook time is complete, drain and add 2 Tablespoons of olive oil to keep them fresh while you are cooking.
2. Brown ground beef. Use a spatula to break off the meat and flip it around until all pieces are browned.
3. Add chopped onion, garlic and green pepper. Cook on medium heat until slightly tender, about four minutes.
4. Add oregano, basil, salt and pepper. Mix thoroughly. Cook on medium heat for one minute.
5. Add diced tomatoes, tomato sauce and tomato paste. Mix thoroughly.
6. Once the mixture has a slight boil to it, turn down the heat to medium-low and simmer on this heat for one hour. Remember to stir often.
7. Add desired sauce to desired noodles.

*Can make ahead of time. Does reheat well. Serves 8-10 people.

Can also make with zucchini noodles, which makes the dish carbohydrate friendly.

Sometimes, we add cheese to the top. Fresh parmesan is great with this!

Turkey Stir Fry

This is one of my favorites, and I have been making it since my oldest children were very little.

2 boil in bag rice (cooked)

2 pounds of ground turkey

3 green peppers (chopped)

2 stalks of fresh broccoli (chopped)

1 cup of green onion (chopped)

1 white onion

1 cup of asparagus

1 cup of soy sauce

3 Tablespoons of brown sugar

2 Tablespoons of canola oil

1. Put soy sauce and brown sugar in a bowl. Stir and let it sit.
2. Add oil to the wok or electric griddle (I like the electric griddle because it cooks everything very evenly). Brown ground turkey until all pieces are cooked through.
3. Add broccoli and chopped peppers. Cook for 3-4 minutes until slightly softened.

4. Add green onion, white onion and asparagus. Cook for 3-4 minutes.
5. Add soy sauce and brown sugar mixture. Cook for 2 minutes.

6. Add 1-2 bags of rice. (If you want to make this with fewer carbohydrates, then you can skip the rice altogether). Cook for 2 minutes.

*You can make this ahead of time. Does reheat well.

Serves 5 people.

All of my children eat this. It is a great way to get kids to eat their vegetables. It is mild and yet delicious!

Pot Roast and Potatoes

This is nice to make on a cold winter day. Also, it makes the house smell amazing all day long while it cooks in the crock pot.

1 Large chuck roast

6 golden potatoes (peeled and cubed into one-inch cubes)

8 Whole carrots (peeled and cut into ½ inch circles)

5 Tablespoons of Thyme

2 Tablespoons of onion powder

2 Tablespoons of garlic powder

2 Tablespoons of celery seed

Salt and pepper to taste

1 cup of beef broth

3 Tablespoons of olive oil

1. 7 hours before you want your meal to be ready, put the crock pot on low. Add the 1 cup of beef broth. Put the chuck roast in the crock pot. Put the lid on the crock pot.
2. Next, add 2 Tablespoons of Thyme, 1 Tablespoon of onion powder, 1 Tablespoon of garlic powder and 1 Tablespoon of celery seed. Again, close the lid when you have completed this task.

3. I like to mix the carrots and potatoes together in a bowl before I put them in the crock pot. This ensures that the spices surround them and cook into them while in the crock pot. Mix carrots, potatoes, 3 Tablespoons of Thyme, 1 Tablespoon of onion powder, 1 Tablespoon of garlic powder and 1 Tablespoon of celery seed. Put 3 Tablespoons of olive oil in the bowl as well. Mix all these ingredients thoroughly. When mixed thoroughly, poor carrot potato mixture on top of the cooking roast.
4. The best part about this meal, is there is nothing else to do until 7 hours after you put the meat in the crock pot. Once 7 hours have passed since the meat was put on low, your meal is delicious and ready. I usually put the crock pot on warm while my family is taking their portions of what they would like.

*You can make it ahead. Does reheat, but the meat might get a little tougher during reheat.

Serves 5 people.

This one really warms the insides as you eat it. Don't forget the extra dash of love!

Hearty Chicken Surprise

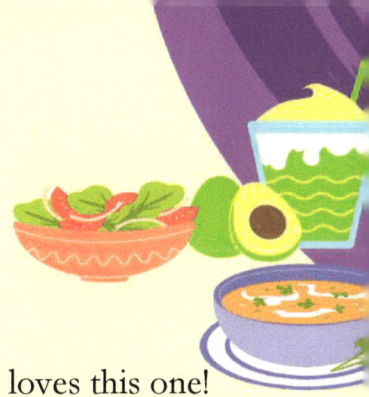

Here is another crock pot dish that is so nice on a cold winter day. My family loves this one!

5 chicken breasts

1 can of Campbell's cream of celery soup

2 cans of Campbell's cream of mushroom soup

1 cup of chicken broth

Salt and pepper to taste

2 bags of boil in the bag rice

1. Put chicken breasts and 1 cup of chicken broth in a crock pot. Put crock pot on low for six hours.
2. After six hours, make boil in a bag rice. Set aside.
3. Shred chicken in broth. You can use two forks to do this.
4. Add cream of celery and cream of mushroom soup to the crock pot. Keep the crock pot on low for an additional 45 minutes.
5. Add rice to the mixture. Add desired salt and pepper.

*You can make it ahead. Does reheat well.

Serves 5 people.

This is super simple and tastes delicious! Enjoy.

Pasta Primavera

This one is really nice if you've got garden veggies to use. It tastes really good all through the year, however.

4 Tablespoons of Weber Garlic Parmesan Seasoning

1 red onion (chopped)

1 zucchini (chopped)

1 yellow squash (chopped)

2 Tablespoons of dried parsley flakes

3 Tablespoons of garlic salt

Penne Pasta to taste

1 ½ cups of broccoli (chopped)

1 green pepper (chopped)

1 red pepper (chopped)

3 Tablespoons of garlic (minced)

8 Tablespoons of canola oil

4 Tablespoons of lemon juice

Fresh Parmesan cheese to taste (I use about 1 ½ cups)

1 cup of grape tomatoes (cut into halves)

1. Cook penne pasta according to the package. Once drained, pour two Tablespoons of canola oil over the pasta so that is stays fresh.
2. In an electric griddle or large pan on medium heat, put 6 Tablespoons of canola oil. Start to saute the broccoli. Add 3 Tablespoons of lemon juice. Continue to saute for about 3 minutes.
3. Add red pepper, green pepper and red onion. Saute for three minutes. Add 3 Tablespoons of garlic. Mix for an additional 2 minutes.
4. Add zucchini and squash. Continue to mix on medium heat for 3 minutes.
5. Add tomato halves. Cook for 3 minutes.
6. Add 4 Tablespoons of Weber Garlic parmesan seasoning, 2 Tablespoons of Parsley Flakes and 3 Tablespoons of Garlic salt. Mix thoroughly.
7. Add the desired amount of pasta to the dish while still heating. Mix thoroughly.
8. Add the desired amount of parmesan cheese. I use about 1 ½ cups. Mix until the cheese is melty.

*You can make it ahead. Does reheat well.

Serves 5-6 people.
Be careful with this one. I can eat a whole plate, and then I want to come back for more. Yummy!

Yummy Garden Surprise

This was inspired by garden picks one year. It turned out very yummy.

4 Tablespoons of olive oil

2 yellow squash (chopped)

1 zucchini (chopped)

2 cubanelle peppers (chopped)

3 green peppers (chopped)

5 Large tomatoes (diced)

4 carnival blend peppers (chopped)

1 albino pepper (chopped)

2 pounds of skirt steak (cut into ½ inch pieces)

Spaghetti noodles to taste

1 cup of fresh parmesan

1 cup of shredded sharp cheddar

1 ½ Tablespoons of lemon juice

2 Tablespoons of Kosher salt

1 Tablespoon of course ground pepper

1 Tablespoon of onion powder

1 cup of tomatoes (diced)

1 Tablespoon of garlic powder

1 ½ Tablespoons of minced onion

1 Tablespoon of celery salt

3 Tablespoons of Weber Garlic Parmesan Seasoning

1. Cook noodles according to package. After straining, add 2 Tablespoons of olive oil to keep fresh while cooking the other ingredients.
2. Add Two Tablespoons of olive oil to an electric griddle or large pan. Cook skirt steak on medium heat until medium rare. Take skirt steak out of the griddle and put it aside.
3. Put yellow squash, zucchini, cubanelle peppers, green peppers, carnival blend peppers and albino pepper in a gridle or pan. Cook on medium heat.
4. Add 2 Tablespoons of Kosher salt, 1 Tablespoon of course ground pepper, 1 Tablespoon of onion powder, 1 Tablespoon of garlic powder, 1 Tablespoon of celery salt, 1 ½ Tablespoons of minced onion and 3 Tablespoons of Weber Garlic Parmesan Seasoning. Mix thoroughly. Cook vegetables until they are slightly tender—about 6 minutes.
5. Add diced tomatoes to the mixture. Cook until tomatoes are starting to break down for about 4 minutes.
6. Add skirt steak back into the mixture and cook for one minute.
7. Add one cup of parmesan and one cup of cheddar cheese. Mix until the cheese is melted.
8. Add the desired amount of noodles to the mixture.

*You can make it ahead. Does reheat well.

Serves 7 people.

If you cannot find all of the specified peppers, you can use red, orange and yellow peppers. This does turn out very good, just as indicated in the recipe.

Katie's Country Skillet

When I made this one for the first time as an idea I had, my partner at the time said, "You need to write that down!" So I did. And here it is.

7 breakfast sausage links (cooked and cut into half-inch circles)

2 cups of golden potatoes (cut into shoestring strips – I use a mandoline to do this)

2 green peppers (chopped)

1 red pepper (chopped)

1 Large white onion (chopped)

4 Eggs (Fried)

1 Teaspoon of onion powder

1 teaspoon of garlic powder

1 teaspoon, of course, ground pepper

Kosher salt to taste

4 Tablespoons of butter

2 Tablespoons of Weber garlic parmesan seasoning

1 ½ cups of shredded chihuahua cheese

1. Melt one Tablespoon of butter. Saute on medium heat diced green pepper, red pepper and onion until they start to get soft. About 3-4 minutes.
2. Add another Tablespoon of butter and shoestring potatoes. Mix on medium heat with all ingredients for about 5 minutes.
3. Add another Tablespoon of butter and continue on medium heat for another 5 minutes.
4. Add 1 teaspoon of onion powder, 1 teaspoon of garlic powder, 1 teaspoon of course ground pepper, Kosher salt to taste and 2 Tablespoons of Weber garlic Parmesan seasoning. Mix thoroughly for 2 minutes.
5. Add the last Tablespoon of butter and also the sausage pieces. Keep stirring thoroughly for 3 minutes.
6. Put mixture into circular Corningware. Put 1 ½ cups of chihuahua cheese on top. Bake at 350 degrees for 15 minutes.
7. During this time, you can fry your four eggs sunny-side up. Put on a plate aside until the baked dish is ready.
8. Serve a portion of the scooped skillet mixture with the desired amount of fried eggs on top.

*Can make ahead of time. However, the eggs will need to be made fresh each time.

Serves 4-5 people.

When those egg yolks break on top of the cheesy skillet mixture…it is so yummy and delicious. Enjoy!

Summer Pasta Salad

This one goes perfectly with grilled meats on a nice summer evening.

¾ cup of olive oil

4 Tablespoons of balsamic vinegar

4 cups of rotini pasta

1 pint of cherry tomatoes (cut in half)

2 balls of fresh mozzarella cheese cut into ½ inch pieces

2 teaspoons of seasoned salt

1 teaspoon, of course, ground pepper

2 Tablespoons dried basil

1 ½ Tablespoons of dried oregano

2 teaspoons of parsley flakes

3 cloves of fresh garlic (pressed to minced)

1 cup of thick-cut salami (cut into ½ inch pieces)

1. Cook pasta according to the package. After straining, drizzle some olive oil and set aside.

2. Mix oil, balsamic vinegar, 2 teaspoons of seasoned salt, 1 teaspoon of course, ground pepper, 2 Tablespoons of dried basil, 1 ½ Tablespoons of dried oregano, 2 teaspoons of parsley flakes and minced garlic. Put aside.
3. You can use a melon scoop to make the mozzarella into small balls. Set aside.
4. Mix pasta, tomatoes, oil spice mixture, cheese and salami. Let sit for 5 minutes, then mix thoroughly again.
5. Chill in the refrigerator for at least 2 hours.

*You can make it ahead. Does not require heating. It is a chilled dish.

Serves 5-6 people.

I love this dish for summer parties like at 4th of July! Being chilled will cool you off on a warm summer day.

Quick and Yummy Chili

This is a very quick and easy way to make a pot of chili. It turns out very nice to accompany a football game.

2 packets of Chili man seasoning

1 Tablespoon of garlic powder

½ Tablespoon of onion powder

1 Tablespoon of Kosher salt

¼ teaspoon garlic salt

2 Tablespoons of minced garlic

1 green pepper (chopped)

1 red pepper (chopped)

1 yellow pepper (chopped)

1 large white onion (chopped)

1 ½ pounds of ground beef

1 16 oz can of red kidney beans

1 teaspoon of course ground pepper

1 Tablespoon of olive oil

28 ounces of crushed tomatoes

16 ounces of tomato sauce

1. Put one Tablespoon of olive oil and green pepper, red pepper, yellow pepper and white onion in the large pot. Put the heat on medium and cook until the onions start to carmelize and become a little brown.
2. In a separate pan, put heat to medium and start to brown the ground beef.
3. Add 2 Tablespoons of minced garlic to the pepper and onion pot. Cook for one additional minute.
4. Once the meat mixture is all browned, drain the fat and add to the pepper and onion pot. Add the two chili man packets, 1 teaspoon, of course, ground pepper, ¼ teaspoon of garlic salt, Kosher salt to taste, 1 Tablespoon of garlic powder and ½ Tablespoon of onion powder. Cook on medium heat for three minutes.
5. Add crushed tomatoes and tomato sauce to the mixture. Cook for three minutes.
6. Add kidney beans to the pot. Mix thoroughly.
7. Cook on low, mixing often for 30 minutes.

*Can make ahead of time. Reheats well.

Serves 5-7 people

This is a really quick and easy way to make a pot of chili. This is tasty and will give some nice nutrients.

Double Cheese Cajun Burgers

If you're looking for a little flare to your everyday burger, this is a nice choice. The recipe only makes two, so if you are looking for more, just double or triple the recipe.

1 pound of ground beef

1 cup of shredded chihuahua cheese

2 slices of American Cheese

1 Tablespoon of cajun seasoning

¼ teaspoon of celery salt

¼ teaspoon of seasoned salt

¼ teaspoon of course ground pepper

2 Hamburger buns

1. Put a pound of ground beef in a bowl and mix with chihuahua cheese, ¾ Tablespoon of cajun seasoning, ¼ teaspoon of celery salt, ¼ teaspoon of seasoned salt, and ¼ teaspoon of course ground pepper. Mix thoroughly. Knead with hands to get all spices evenly distributed.
2. Form patties. After the patties are formed, sprinkle the remaining cajun seasoning on each burger.
3. Grill patties to taste. I like them medium rare. Add American cheese to the outside of the burger when almost completely cooked through.

4. After taking the burger off of the grill, toast the buns on the burger grease to get a nice little toast for your buns.

*You can make it ahead, but it does not reheat as well as when originally made.

Serves 2 people.

Can also top with pepper jack cheese instead of American.

This is a bit spicy – so if you don't like spice, you won't like this.

Katie's Fish Stew

When I made this one, I immediately wrote down the recipe because I liked it so much. So did my partner.

½ cup of lemon juice

4 Tablespoons of fish sauce

4 Tilapia fillets

2 Tablespoons minced onion (dried)

2 Tablespoons of oregano

4 Tablespoons of Weber Garlic Parmesan Seasoning

2 Tablespoons of basil

3 Tablespoons of onion powder

1 ½ Tablespoons of dried chives

2 Tablespoons of garlic powder

4 Tablespoons of dried, dehydrated garlic minced

7 Tablespoons of olive oil

1 Tablespoon of Kosher salt

1 teaspoon of pepper

Salt and pepper to taste for tilapia filet

10 Roma Tomatoes (diced)

1 green pepper (diced)

3 red peppers (diced)

1 Large white onion (chopped)

4 Cubanelle peppers (chopped)

2 anneheim peppers (chopped)

1 Pablano pepper (diced)

1 Giant red Marconi pepper (diced)

1. Put ½ cup of lemon juice, 4 Tablespoons of fish sauce, 2 Tablespoons of dehydrated onions, 2 Tablespoons of oregano, 4 Tablespoons of Weber Garlic Parmesan Seasoning, 2 Tablespoons of Basil, 3 Tablespoons of onion powder, 1 ½ Tablespoons of dried chives, 2 Tablespoons of garlic powder, 4 Tablespoons of dehydrated garlic, 3 Tablespoons of olive oil, 1 Tablespoon of Kosher salt, 1 Teaspoon of pepper, 10 Roma tomatoes, green pepper, red pepper, onion, cubanelle peppers, anaheim peppers, poblano pepper and giant red Marconi in a large saucepan. Heat on medium and stir frequently. Tomatoes will help form a liquid, and the liquid will start to bubble to a boil. Keep on medium heat and keep stirring frequently.
2. While the stew is cooking, get tilapia ready for a pan fry—season tilapia with salt and pepper to taste.
3. Put 4 Tablespoons of olive oil in a pan and fry 4 Tilapia fillets until they are white and cooked through. I usually flip them every 3 minutes. Usually takes a total of about 8 minutes.
4. Remember to keep stirring stew with all the veggies frequently.
5. Cut tilapia into inch-size pieces.
6. Taste the stew and once the peppers are soft, add tilapia pieces to the stew. The total cook time on the stew is going to be about 15-20 minutes. Mix thoroughly. Then, take off the heat and serve warm.

*You can make it ahead. Can reheat.

Serves 7 people.

If you can not find all of these different kinds of peppers, you can put some yellow and orange peppers in as well. This is a very tasty dish – I hope you enjoy it!

Stuffed Pablano and Giant Red Marconi Peppers

This was a recipe I came up with while experimenting with some garden picks. Myself and my partner really enjoyed it, so I wrote down the recipe.

2 cups of shredded chihuahua cheese

1 teaspoon of carmelized onion butter seasoning

1 teaspoon of course ground pepper

1 Tablespoon of cajun seasoning

1 ½ teaspoon of paprika

3 Tablespoons of Italian seasoning

1 ½ teaspoons of Kosher salt

1 Tablespoon of Weber Garlic Parmesan seasoning

3 Roma tomatoes (diced)

3 red peppers (diced)

3 Tablespoons of minced garlic

1 Large white onion (chopped)

1 pound of 85% lean ground beef

3 Large Pablano Peppers (to stuff) (cut into halves)

3 Large Giant Red Marconi Peppers (to stuff) (cut into halves)

1 ½ Tablespoons of olive oil

1. Put olive oil in a large pan. Put heat on medium. Add red peppers and onion and cook for 3 minutes.
2. Add tomato and garlic and cook on medium heat for another 3 minutes.
3. Cook until the peppers are malleable. It should take about 6-8 minutes total.
4. Put vegetable mixture aside. Put ground beef in the same pan. Cook until browned throughout. Use a spatula to break up meat and turn it as you cook it.
5. Once the meat is browned, add 1 teaspoon of carmelized onion butter, 1 teaspoon, of course, ground pepper, 1 Tablespoon of cajun seasoning, 1 ½ teaspoons of paprika, 3 Tablespoons of Italian seasoning, 1 ½ teaspoon of Kosher salt and 1 Tablespoon of Weber Garlic Parmesan seasoning. Mix into meat thoroughly.
6. Add the vegetable mixture back into the pan with the meat and seasoning mixture. Cook on medium heat for 2 minutes, then remove from heat.
7. Take halved poblano and giant red Marconi peppers and place them on a foil-lined baking sheet to put on the grill. (Grilling a cookie sheet will ruin it for other cooking purposes, but it is great for cooking things like this on the grill.) Fill the halves of the peppers with the meat and vegetable mixture.
8. Grill on medium heat (about 400 degrees) until the halved peppers have charred and softened a bit. This will take about 8-10 minutes.
9. Put shredded chihuahua cheese on top of the halved stuffed peppers. Grill until cheese is melted. This will take 3-4 minutes.

*You can make it ahead. Does reheat well.

Serves 6 people.

This is a fun recipe for a cookout with friends! I'm licking my lips thinking about this one.

Sausage Stir Fry

If you haven't been able to tell, I love mixing veggies, proteins and other fun ingredients into a stir fry. This one packs a punch of flavor.

2 Tablespoons of olive oil

Andoulli sausage to taste (I use one package, which is about 16 ounces) (cut into ½ inch circular pieces)

1 cup of shredded Colby cheese

1 cup of shredded pepper jack cheese

1 red pepper (diced)

1 yellow pepper (diced)

1 orange pepper (diced)

1 boil in bag rice (cooked)

1 Tablespoon of paprika

4 Tablespoons of Weber Garlic Parmesan seasoning

Salt and pepper to taste (the sausage can be salty, so taste while adding salt)

1 cup of green onion (chopped both the green and white parts of the onion)

1 red onion (chopped)

3 Tablespoons of minced garlic

1 cup of red pickled beets (chopped into ½ inch pieces)

¾ cup of celery (chopped)

2 Tablespoons of dried chives

1 Tablespoon of fish sauce

2 Tablespoons of lime juice

1 green pepper (diced)

1. Put 2 Tablespoons of olive oil in a large skillet. I use an electric griddle because the veggies and cooked items have an even space to cook. You can use a wok or other large pan as well. Cook andoulli sausage pieces on medium heat (325 degrees on an electric griddle) until they are slightly browned. Take the sausage out and put it aside.
2. Cook celery, green pepper, red pepper, yellow pepper, orange pepper, green onion and red onion on medium heat until slightly softened. Cook about 4 minutes.
3. If the mixture is dry, add another Tablespoon of oil. Then add garlic, chives, 1 Tablespoon of paprika, 4 Tablespoons of garlic parmesan seasoning, fish sauce and lime juice. Cook for 3 minutes.
4. Add beets and sausage to the mixture. Cook for 2 minutes.
5. Add salt and pepper to taste.
6. Add cooked rice. Stir until mixed thoroughly.
7. Add Colby and pepperjack cheese and cook until cheese is melted. This will take about 2-3 minutes.

*You can make it ahead. Does reheat well.

Serves 7-8 people.

The sausage in this really adds a lot of fun to the dish. Another reason I love stir fry is that once the preparation of cutting the vegetables is done, it doesn't take that long for a delicious dish.

Desserts

Cinnamon Crumb Banana Bread

OR

Strawberry Banana Bread

I've been making banana bread since I was in college. This cinnamon crumb banana bread evolved over time and became a delicious addition to our dessert menu.

1 cup of strawberries (chopped)

OR

2 Tablespoons of cinnamon (cinnamon crumble ingredients and directions will be listed below)

2 cups of flour

¾ teaspoon of baking soda

½ teaspoon of salt

¾ cup of sugar

6 Tablespoons of butter (slightly melted)

2 Eggs

1 cup of mashed bananas (this is about 2 large extra ripe bananas)

¼ cup of water

Cinnamon Crumble ingredients

1 stick and 2 Tablespoons of butter (melted)

1 cup of flour

¼ cup of brown sugar

¼ cup of white sugar

1 Tablespoons of cinnamon

If making the cinnamon crumble recipe, mix all cinnamon crumble ingredients and sprinkle on top of the bread mixture before placing it in the oven.

1. Grease and flour a 9x5 metal loaf pan.
2. Mix flour, baking soda and salt. Set aside.
3. In a separate bowl, mix slightly melted butter, sugar and eggs. Blend with mixer for five minutes. It should appear creamy when done. Set aside.
4. In another separate bowl, mix mashed bananas and water.
5. Put mashed bananas and water mixture into the bowl with butter, sugar and eggs. Blend with mixer for one minute.
6. Slowly add flour, baking soda and salt mixture.
7. IF making strawberry banana bread, add strawberries. OR IF making cinnamon crumble banana bread, add cinnamon. Blend for 1 minute.
8. Poor batter into a greased and floured loaf pan. If making cinnamon crumble banana bread, add the crumble recipe on top.

9. The oven should be set to 350 degrees. Strawberry banana bread is baked for 63 minutes. Cinnamon crumble recipe bakes for 60-70 minutes. When the bread is almost ready, check with a toothpick. Stick a toothpick down the highest point to ensure that the bread is thoroughly baked. Some ovens bake a little differently.

*You can make it ahead.

Serves 7-9 people.

These are favorites in our household. My older children love banana bread.

Apple Crisp

This recipe I usually make in the Fall when the apples near us are ripe. My partner, at the time I started this recipe, absolutely loved it and asked me to write it down.

10 cups green apples (peeled, cored and sliced)

2 ½ cups of white sugar

1 ¼ cup and 1 Tablespoon of flour

¼ cup and 1 Tablespoon of cinnamon

½ cup of water

1 cup of cooking oats

1 cup of brown sugar

1 ½ cups of melted butter

¼ teaspoon of baking powder

¼ teaspoon of baking soda

1. Put sliced apples in a 9x13 baking dish.
2. Mix 1 cup of white sugar, 1 Tablespoon of flour and ¼ cup of cinnamon. Mix this into the apples. Poor ½ cup of water around the edge of the apples.

3. Mix 1 cup of oats, 1 ¼ cups of flour, 1 cup of brown sugar, 1 Tablespoon of cinnamon, ¼ teaspoon of baking powder, ¼ teaspoon of baking soda, 1 ½ cups of melted butter and 1 ½ cups of white sugar together. Crumble this mixture over the apples in the 9x5 baking dish.
4. Bake at 350 degrees for 45 minutes.

(Apples will be soft, and crumble will be like a crust)

*You can make it ahead. Does reheat well. Eats well cold, too.

Serves 11-12 people

I try to share this dish as much as possible when I make it because I can eat the whole 9x5 dish. It's very nice to accompany a fall dinner party.

www.ingramcontent.com/pod-product-compliance
Lightning Source LLC
Chambersburg PA
CBHW061140030426
42335CB00002B/48